MY NONFICTION DECODABLE READERS

Up to Us Kids

BY KIM THOMPSON

A Little Honey Book

Crabtree Publishing
crabtreebooks.com

Tips for Teachers and Caregivers

This book supports early readers as they decode words to learn facts and gain knowledge about the world.

Before reading, make sure students understand the sound-spelling correspondences shown below as well as the high-frequency words shown on the next page. Introduce the vocabulary words.

During reading, provide feedback and encouragement as students sound out decodable words by blending individual sounds.

After reading, talk about and write about the topic. Share the information on page 16 to help students learn more.

Letters and Sounds

New:

Sound	Spelling
/k/	ck
/k/	k
short u	u

Review:

Sound	Spelling
short a	a
/b/	b
/k/	c
/d/	d
/f/	f
/g/	g
/h/	h
short i	i
/m/	m
/n/	n
short o	o
/p/	p
/r/	r
/s/	s
/t/	t

Decodable Words

and, back, Bud, can, fun, fuss, in, is, it, Kat, kick, kids, Kim, kits, Kudrick, mad, Mick, Miss, mud, nuts, pick, run, sacks, sun, tug, up, us

High-Frequency Words

New: again, been, have, jump, likes, says, time, what

Review: a, for, get, good, more, no, the, to, we

Vocabulary Words

craft

tie

tug-of-war

Miss Kudrick says we have been good.

We get time for fun.

What can we pick?

It is up to us kids.

Quarter III
Character Learning Targets

Kat says **tug-of-war**.

Mick likes to run and kick.

Bud likes to jump in sacks.

Kim is nuts for **craft** kits!

We pick. It is a **tie**.

Kids fuss. Kids get mad.

"Back up," says Miss Kudrick.

"We can pick again."

"Tug-of-war is more fun," Kat says. "We can tug in the mud!"

“No,” Bud says. “A sack is more fun. We can jump in the Sun!”

We pick again.

The kids like tug-of-war.

We have fun!

Build Background Knowledge

It can be challenging to work together to make a decision that is good for everyone in a group. Rules and procedures help each person feel included and respected. People in authority can make sure that rules are followed. Each member of a classroom community has an important role to play. How does a decision about a fun-time activity get made in this classroom? Is it fair? How does the teacher help?

MY NONFICTION DECODABLE READERS

UP TO US KIDS

Written by: Kim Thompson
Designed by: Rhea Magaro
Series Development: James Earley
Educational Consultant: Marie Lemke, M.Ed.

Photographs: All images from Shutterstock

Crabtree Publishing

crabtreebooks.com 800-387-7650

Printed in China/012024/FE20231222

Published in Canada
Crabtree Publishing
616 Welland Ave.
St. Catharines, Ontario
L2M 5V6

Published in the United States
Crabtree Publishing
347 Fifth Ave
Suite 1402-145
New York, NY 10016

Library and Archives Canada Cataloguing in Publication
Available at Library and Archives Canada

Library of Congress Cataloging-in-Publication Data
Available at the Library of Congress

Hardcover: 978-1-0398-4432-2
Paperback: 978-1-0398-4513-8
Ebook (pdf): 978-1-0398-4590-9
Epub: 978-1-0398-4660-9
Read-Along: 978-1-0398-4730-9
Audio: 978-1-0398-4800-9